THOUGHTS and POETRY on PAPER

PETER KNOESTER

 FriesenPress

One Printers Way
Altona, MB R0G 0B0
Canada

www.friesenpress.com

ISBN
978-1-03-833777-1 (Hardcover)
978-1-03-833776-4 (Paperback)
978-1-03-833778-8 (eBook)

1. BIOGRAPHY & AUTOBIOGRAPHY, RELIGIOUS

Distributed to the trade by The Ingram Book Company

RELIGIOUS THOUGHTS, STORIES AND POETRY

FOREWORD

I t's true enough that these my thoughts and opinions on things, are of a religious nature. But it is also true that in it are segments pertaining to every day life, that in one way or another affect us all. I realize that it is an odd mixture, but then again, why not. The person reading this book may see the different aspects of live and see another side, than the more conventional way. The one hope I have is this, that through this book I may enlighten a few people and to make others aware that they are not alone in their thoughts or state of mind. It is not my goal to convert anyone to my way of thinking, only to open a door through which a person may enter in and see a different world than the one that he or she may be use to. It may seem that some of the things written are of a repetitive nature, but some things need to be repeated in order to stick in our mind. There is an urge in most of us to leave something behind after we are gone, to be remembered by, for me it are the things I wrote about, may it be to good use even if it is only for one person. At and during the time that I wrote this, I was diagnosed as having a growth in my liver the size of a small orange, one could well imagine the fear that came over me and the anguish among the family members, because of the possibilities of it being cancerous. I did try to prepare myself for the worst but what can one do but pray. The realities of life and death I started to be aware of, like a garment that one puts on every day. It took several weeks to finally have an biopsy done, as one has to wait for an opening and is placed on a waiting list. You can well understand our relieve after being told that the growth was benign but to keep an eye out and have it looked at every six months We are all grateful to our Maker who granted me an extension on life. To some these writings may look amateurish with a grammar that is full of flaws and the sentences too long etc. But that is me and I mean well and I hope you will enjoy and understand the things written as well as the poetry

I would like to dedicate this work to my wife Catherine who passed away on the 22nd of May 2003 and put up with me all those years.

MY THOUGHTS ON THE DEATH OF PRINCESS DIANA

The terrible news of Princess Diana's death came as a shock to the whole world. Who could ever have thought that this gentle creature, that was so beloved by everyone would die, in such a violent accident at the young age of thirty-six. Needless to say that her marriage to Prince Charles, which was watched on television by probably one billion people, made her the Princess of the storybook, "The Fairy Princess." This imprint of her has never left the people's mind. To them, she will always be that lovely creature in her beautiful wedding gown. Our hearts go out at this time to the two sons that this marriage produced, and we sincerely hope that their grief is bearable and that God is their strength. It is a pity that this marriage did not last.

What happened, no one can really tell, because you'll only know a person after you have lived with him or her for a while? Most people lay the blame at Prince Charlie's door, which in a way, is not fair because, while Diana was very out spoken, Prince Charles could not be, because he was tied down by tradition and protocol. We can see that the almost ultra modern Diana, which she became in later years, was more than a match for the somewhat overly rigid future Monarch, who was thirteen years her senior. There is some that say that Charles never has experienced the parental love that most ordinary children receive, and therefore may not have been able to express his own love to others. Whatever the reason, to most people, the break up of this marriage was a bitter disappointment. Diana stayed in the glare of the media lights and went to a lot of functions of one sort or another, and traveled around the world during the last few years of her life, doing a lot of charity work and did show a genuine interest in the helpless, the disabled and the mentally disadvantaged and was not averse to coming in contact with people that had diseases, like aids, or leprosy. By doing all these things she had even become more beloved then she had been before. One thing is certain, because she kinned herself as it were, to the common people, she will be missed by everyone. Whether she will become an icon, I don't know. I hope not, for she, in my opinion, would not approve. The outpouring of love for her by the British people especially, I can only compare to the song "Lilly Marlene," which was sung by both sides during the Second World War, and brought tears to the eyes of many a war weary soldier, because it reminded him of home and family. I will never forget the heartrending cries of many of the people that had been waiting for so many hours along the route that the burial party would take, expressing their sorrow over the death of Diana. I for one will miss her.

THOUGHTS ABOUT THE BEGINNING

"To write or not to write that is the question?" Whether it makes the mind (because what is a person, but a mind on legs?); "nobler" to relieve itself from knowledge and to impart to others, things experienced and learned through reading and hearing. Whether in part true, or all true, depends on the person doing it. We as human beings have a tendency to make ourselves more than what we actually are and have an ability to make a lie look awfully like the truth. The more mentally agile people can adapt themselves to any given situation more readily than a person who is basically slower witted, at least compared to the ones that are more mentally agile. I believe that everybody is endowed with a specialty of some sort. Even the mentally disadvantaged have a certain trait that comes to the fore, when they become older, it is an ability in something, that is not always obvious, call it a gift from the Almighty. There are people who don't seem to have a gift of any kind, but are kind, loving, caring and have charity toward others. Beware of those, as they could be angels that we meet unawares. The very traits mentioned are _The Gifts_ because anyone possessing these, is Gods favourite, He will come to their aid and will not allow that evil is spoken of them without retaliation.

It is true that the mind of mankind is such, that it constantly will try to please itself with all the pleasant feelings, whether it is a beautiful view or a caress, sex, good food, or pleasant conversations with others, music, etc. In other words, anything that pleases the five senses: hearing, seeing, feeling, tasting and smelling.

As far as the sixth sense is concerned, I believe the sixth to be the feeling of a general well being, a satisfaction with ones lot, although people call it ESP (extra sensory perception), a kind of not knowing but still knowing through faith or mental perception. In women it is called intuition, something that is known intuitively without knowing why they know. The brain (mind) is the greatest computer ever created by The Master Builder.

It will never be equalled by modern technology, whatever they will try. The brain is a sponge, especially in the stage shortly after birth, although it does experience a lot of things in the womb, mostly sound like things. Needless to say that if the foetus experiences harsh sounds and loud arguments and fights amongst a household, it will be affected adversely and have stamped on it's mind, a trait that in later life or even immediately after birth is detrimental to the development of a loving, caring human being.

It is my firm belief that children from broken homes suffer from these traits, but not exclusively.

I don't think that there are very many people on this planet that would not hold a belief that there are good and evil forces at work in this world. We are beset by them in all areas, one has only to read a book to find out there are good and bad characters also in movies and of course most of all in real life, our own. How many times don't we hear others and also ourselves say; "I don't like this or that person?" Usually it is because something was said or done that bruised our ego by that person, by word or deed and the inability to forgive or to forget about the incident is not there. Therefore, the event is stored in the brain and every time we see that person the mind reminds us and a bitter hatred for that person ensues, and it will become a vicious circle, out of which we cannot escape unless we forgive that person, who half the time does not know why you act so hostile toward him or her. Nowadays there are psychoanalysts that understand the workings of the brain through study, via Freud and others, and charge a fee to impart their knowledge to people who don't know how to forgive their partners, family members, former friends, so they are shown how to overcome that giant ego that is their own nemesis and to make themselves more loving, kinder and charitable.

There are not many things that succeed without discipline. A child growing up without knowing discipline will grow up wild, without bounds set by discipline. A person overstepping certain bounds in a society will soon become an outcast or become incarcerated, if the boundaries of social behaviour are overstepped too grossly and are deemed to be criminal by his peers.

From the most primitive tribes of Africa to the most modern countries in the world, there are groups of people and sometimes entire countries that have adopted one kind of religion or other, to not only keep the masses in check, but also to ensure that people do not destroy one another because of bruised egos. All that is said or written until now is just a general view of what individuals or societies are all about. Mankind unlike animals is aware of their mortality. The question, "Why am I on this earth," has come out of many a mouth. It is very hard to deny that a higher force is at work in the universe to keep everything from collapsing, and seeing and having overcome the hurdle of denying that possibility, it follows that there is a purpose for our existence. I would like to impart to the reader, of this epistle what I believe this purpose to be.

I am of the Judean-Christian Faith, a Protestant, brought up in a family that followed after The Calvinistic - Lutheran teachings, in which household, the Bible was read after every meal and before going to bed to retire for the night. Most of the time I was an unwilling participant, head-strong and full of worldly know-how not realizing that my father's duty in life, was to make sure that his children were taught the way to salvation, by reading from the "good book," as they say, that way his children would get to know the way to such a wondrous and spectacular salvation through Jesus Christ. But let me not jump ahead from what I was about to write.

The Bible starts by saying, "that in the beginning, God created heaven and earth." When that beginning was, nobody knows, except God and if it were told to us, we could not possibly comprehend it. I believe that God the Father, God the Son, and their Holy Spirit are without begin-ning, without end, all powerful, omnipotent, totally creative, loving and righteous without a blemish of any kind, perfect in every way with mind power (for lack of a better description) so tremendously that even the most "powerful" computer ever built, or still being built is but a mental midget compared to this Trinity in one. I believe that in the beginning everything was created, from galaxies and universes, every planet, moon and star, all angels and all the souls of men, but who has seen God's mind or to whom would God reveal his intentions? Therefore, who am I to try to interpret or to reveal something unknown to all mankind. Therefore, I should tell my mind to be still and to leave well enough alone. At this point the Bible stories should take over and the interpretation should be left to whom God has revealed it, first Jesus the Christ who was there and told all from first hand experience and then through the Holy Spirit by others, first the

RELIGIOUS THOUGHTS, STORIES AND POETRY

Apostles of whom Paul was the most informed through the Spirit, then through the ages by the from God called preachers, teachers, prophets etc. to this present day. There is no doubt in my mind that we are living in the latter days and that shortly must come to pass that of which was spoken of by the prophets of long ago, blood, fire and smoke. Blessed will be those that are already asleep and blessed will be those whom God has appointed to escape these calamities to come, by the "Rapture" to meet the Saviour in the air and there to wait until all that God has said that would come to pass, has occurred and then come triumphant with Christ to take possession of the earth and bind the dragon (Satan) and throw him and his angels into the bottomless pit to be bound for a thousand years.

Death will be swallowed up because of a victorious Christ who through his willingness to come down from heaven and to die like a criminal, so that part of the people that ever lived from the beginning of creation would be saved through saving grace and receive eternal life everlasting. All this is because God so loved the world (mankind) that he did not spare His only begotten Son, who on the cross took all our sins great and small on Himself and died in agony, the price for us sinners, so that we through Him would be washed clean from every sin committed and through no effort or deed on our side, beget eternal life through the born again experience which is the implant of God's Spirit in our hearts and thus becoming a (true Christian) or a "little Christ" and is looked upon by God as adopted children through Christ our Lord.

RELIGIOUS THOUGHTS

The spring of 1997 seems to have taken its time coming, although in early April we had almost a week of above normal warm weather. Unfortunately this dissipated and winter came back with a vengeance, covering the countryside again with snow and temperatures way below normal. We already had seen robins on the front lawn that had to suffer through another mini winter with temperatures dropping to well below 0 C. We had to have the driveway ploughed several times, as our vehicles were not able to make the hill (driveway). It will be the first spring that my dad will miss in 87 years, as he was born April 12, 1910 and passed away the night of the 22nd of November. I miss the man, as I did love my Dad and would have died for him if it had been necessary to do so to save his life. Unfortunately, this is not possible as we as human beings are destined to depart from this world when our, "time is up" as they say. Oh how I wrestle with this happening, this event, that can only be likened to a holy moment as the soul departs from this body to be with its Maker It's hard for an earthly person to understand what eternity really is. It's the same as talking about light years and the distances of the universes that are farther away then our own Milky Way, we can just barely imagine what it means, let alone understand with our limited brain capacity.

I believe the eye to be the most powerful tool in our arsenal that has pretty well the same speed as a thought has in visualization as in thinking back in time to another place. A thought can cover thousands of miles in a fraction of a second, and even if one is not there physically, we are there in thought. The eye has a more direct, a moment to moment (although always in the present) ability to look into the past especially when looking at distances, even short ones. If I look into the sky above me on a clear night and see the moon and the stars, I am actually looking into the past and it is possible that the star that I am looking at is already gone for some reason or another, as everything has a life expectancy. Even things that are, let say under a mile away, like an animal, whether it is a horse or a cow or any other creature, because it takes time for an image to come from the object into the eye and then having to be interpreted by the brain as to what the eye sees. Ergo, we are looking into the past because the object has moved a fraction of an inch from the time we see it, ergo, we don't see a true picture as it were.

I realize it is a futile thing to write about, even if it has an interesting side to it, because there is no end to it and everything can be philosophized away or into existence. Even the Pharaohs of Egypt had a vision that as they passed on they would become a star in the Orion Constellation and live until all eternity. We all, as human beings, have an outlook into things eternal. The one says this and another that. To me it is no secret as such, but rather obvious in many ways that there is a Creator who passed the way to salvation (eternal life) onto His oracle people, the descendants of Abraham, the "Israelites" of which came to "Torah" where we got the Old Testament from to which later was added the New Testament, now our Bible, in there can be found the way to eternal life if we with God's help and the help of his Holy Spirit can be made to understand that wonderful ideal, that can be ours by grace.

ABOUT CHRIST

When I was first born and suckled my mother's breasts, was I then innocent, sweet and harmless without sin? There is some truth in this, although I already wore the cloak of the "fallen man" the stigma of Adam and Eve. Even then I needed forgiveness of sins and innocence was only a word, even then my life was an open book to Him that caused me to come into the world to do that for which I was appointed, to hurt, love, hate and destroy. To do all that for which the Creator has set boundaries, no more, no less. The notion that birth into a family is purely by chance is a notion that quickly must be put to right. There is nothing in this world that happens by accident, not even the slightest lift of our little finger. Everything has been preordained. The future unrolls itself like a scroll. There is no deviation from it except perhaps through prayer. We may believe we can alter the future through prayer or change something in it. Like Hezekiah when he was dying and asked God for an extension on his life, or when during the battle, Moses arms where held up by Aaron and Hur in order to prevail over the enemy or the time when God was asked to make the daylight last longer in order to defeat all of the enemy, but in the end it had to be so. Another proof of preordination is what God says Himself; "Jacob have I loved but Esau have I hated," and that while they were still in the womb. This, in my point of view is proof that God already had seen the end results of both lives.

Needless to say that all those prophecies prophesied by the seers of old until the present day, are all without fail coming to pass. They could see into the future as to what was going to be at the set times. If these events were not going to happen in the future, the seers could not have seen them of old. They would be looking into a void. We are in this world because we are part of the universe ever since creation or even before, when all the spirits were still with God and separation had not taken place. Maybe that is the reason that in some of us there is a longing to become united again with the well of all life and happiness, realizing that the absence is just temporary.

But now because of Adam there is a barrier between the Creator and His Creation which can only be breached through the belief in the mediator Jesus Christ and his atoning work through which as many as are chosen through and according to his mercy will attain access to the Father, as Christ is the door, through which we may enter into that realm that was prepared for us from the beginning of time. Religion should not be a hard to understand dogma, with oppressing rules and regulations. It should be simplicity itself, to be understood by the most simple minded, without difficulty. Christ's parable of the "sower" or preacher, is man's hope eternal. If the light that's in the word shines in our hearts as we walk along the road of life in this darkened world, we may through grace complete our journey and receive the crown of glory because He loved us so. We know the road is darkened because of Adam's disobedience to his Maker and because of that, we are all tainted and through our actions proof that we are the descendants of him that listened to Satan. Pain and suffering, wars and all manner of diseases has become our portion and if it was not for God's love for His creation, we would have no hope, but now we do and the sun of righteousness has gone up over mankind and His words spoken more than two thousand years ago are tugging on our heart strings to persuade us to follow Him while saying, my yoke is light and the burden small, compared with eternity and all that this entails. The simplicity of the Judean-Christian religion is most essential to the hearer or reader and all unnecessary expansion should be avoided as it would distract from the ultimate goal of bringing into captivity those people who are through God's grace chosen to be with Him in all eternity through the sacrifice of His Son the Saviour. If we only were to understand God's plan for mankind in part, it would make us stand in awe. Most people either don't recognize the Creator for what He is and His omnipotence, the mystery of the Alpha and the Omega, the Beginning and the End which means the beginning of time and the end of time which in itself is incomprehensible and are only words in our vocabulary. Who can understand or fathom the mind of God and who is able to stand before Him without a sponsor, the Redeemer, who through His suffering and death on the cross has fulfilled His Father's wish because He loved us so. So you see that God did not even spare His only Son but gave Him over to this world, this realm where Satan reigns, for a short season. Again, in this is proof that these things had to come to pass because it was ordained by the Almighty to be so.

The promises to Adam to Abraham to Isaac to Jacob to Joseph, Judah's Linage, to David, then to Joseph and Maria, culminated with Christ's birth, heralded by the angels themselves. That must have been something to hear. We as human kind are prone to want proof of most things. We may even dare to challenge God Himself for proof for this or that, we don't know what we do or say, it's like the pot asking the potter "why have you made me like this?" God is true to His word because He only is righteous and true and all of mankind are a lying lot. There are those that actually believe that everything happened by chance. The theory of evolution they call it, these poor creatures don't realize that by advocating this, they deny the God head and are making void the word of God and slander his Majesty and trod on the Messiah by whom all was created ("The Word") and because of this, cannot find a way of escape through Christ our Lord and Saviour. As mentioned earlier, religion as a basis of honouring the Creator, started already in paradise by Adam revering his Creator as he communicated with him. Religion is basically a spiritual thing more than anything else is. Religion is a way to the ultimate goal, to be with our Maker our Creator, from whom we were separated, because of the intervention of Satan in the garden of Eden, (Eden means "Heart of God") and the consequent "Falling" of Adam and Eve and their being driven out of the garden. Now, because of these events, all mankind through Adam and Eve are separated from God. I don't need to write down all the events that took place since then; they are in the bible. Suffice to say that because of God's nature, man could not come close to him without being harmed and all manners of laws had to be observed. God spoke to His appointed people directly or through dreams, even when He talked to Moses through the burning bush that had attracted Moses curiosity, Moses had to take off the shoes from off his feet to honour his Maker. When the Israelites came out of Egypt after all the miracles that had taken place He showed Himself in a column of smoke by day and column of fire by night. This must also have been really something to see. Later on, God thought it better to "dwell" among the people of Israel and ordered a Tabernacle to be made according to precise dimensions with all it's paraphernalia to use a common word and the Ark of the Covenant (which was a substitute for Christ) with it's precise dimensions and adornments as a token not only of God's willingness to dwell among His people but also that the promises made of old would come to pass as He is honest and true who will make it happen.

Then God's love for His people was manifested by the giving of the ten commandments as a rule to live by, having a dual purpose, physically and spiritually. It's obvious if we were, as people (the human race) to live according to these ten commandments the world would be an ideal place, unfortunately for mankind it is also a spiritual law that can only be fulfilled by One in whom all the nations would be blessed that is, the chosen ones from all nations, kindred's and tongues. So you see that Adam from a blessed state, became accursed and brought death upon mankind, but God in His love for His creation gave him the promise of the mediator between God and man. God gave the law and the curse of it later and used it to be a taskmaster to Christ, because we can not fulfill this law and those who through the Spirit are made to see that inability, will be driven without rest to His Son who only through His atoning work can free us from the curse of "The Law" which carries the death penalty for everyone of us. We will always be like the murmuring Israelites and have to be driven with the whip to our own salvation the whip being "The Law". Our minister said once that when God reveals himself to a person, that person finds that he has always had his back to Him, realizing this, it must be a wonder in many an eye that anyone becomes a born again Christian. Everything has to fall away in that person, nothing may be left, he must deny himself and die himself and become a helpless and hopeless worm with nothing left, totally abased on his knees before his Maker, with no expectations except hope in Gods promises and faith in Him who has said that He will not put out a smoking flax stem or brake off a bruised reed. Faith encompasses everything, it is a combination of expectations, hope and sure knowledge that He who has promised all the things pertaining to the acquirement of eternal life will bring us to His Son, who is the door, through the Holy Spirit, so that we may receive an implant of His eternal undying Spirit and through this, be in Him and He in us and walk through this life with the sureness through faith in His word, into eternal life. Amen.

ABOUT CREATION
AND TIME

When my thoughts go out into the realm of nature and I see the beauty of creation. The flawlessness of how everything is perfectly formed from the smallest blade of grass to the tallest tree. This perfection existed from the beginning of time when the worlds were spoken into existence by the voice of Him who loved us before the worlds were formed. It is something quite unfathomable to understand from our human perspective that everything that is now was also at the beginning. Even things that are being burned at this very moment were already at the beginning. The very blood in our veins (as in moisture) was also at the beginning. Everything we see is just a different form of energy. The very stones in our driveway or on a gravel road are from the beginning of time, whether they were in a molten state or as atomic particles or even gaseous form, does not matter, they were there at the "beginning" in one form or another. So you see nothing can be added or taken away from anything that was created by the Almighty. It boggles the mind when these things are thought on and then we come to the conclusion that whatever is, was before, and what is to come has already been, ergo, our lives are predetermined and only the passing of time will bring this to pass. I belief time to be a human invention, because basically time does not exist. The rotation of the Planets around the sun and the set times of the moon and the deterioration of our body cells, which causes us to age is seemingly proof to us that there is a time for everything and we apply that time in a practical application and call a day (one of earth's rotations) twenty-four hours and from there to, weeks, months, years, etc., and like the good book says, when we are really strong, eighty years is a good old age. But what is eighty years compared to the age of the universe which according to some scientists is still expanding and the expression of "Hundreds of Light Years" is a hard thing to understand and comprehend and makes us feel quite insignificant. I guess when these thoughts enter in, we feel abased and small and are almost compelled to give honour to Him that created it all, and show respect to everything that was created including our fellow man. Unfortunately, the bible teaches us that we as a people have an inborn dislike toward our fellow man and God.

It may not show for years and years but one day at one unguarded moment it shows itself, giving proof that we although created in perfection, did leave our first love, our Creator and listened to the one that was and is the cause of all misery in the world today. Needless to say that we lost everything including our first home called Eden or Paradise. I truly believe that the whole world was paradise, but that particular piece of property was where God met with man on a daily basis. We in our ignorance may well say that if we had been Adam we would not have listened to that evil one, but that may be only after the fact, now that we know what the consequences were of Adam and Eve's actions.

We must understand that Adam knew no evil and was as a little child, ignorant of danger. It was an easy thing for Satan to persuade Adam through Eve because he was in a state of innocence. Only God knows the reason for creation and the fall of Adam, it is all one, no beginning and no end, like a circle, who can tell where the circle starts or where it ends. It is my belief that the Creator knew that this cherub in heaven, this master of music, this morning star, would think at one point that he was a God himself and raised himself above that for which he was intended and ruined God's creation of man and the world, that was so beautiful. As God is perfection, He could not have a relationship with something that was imperfect. There was now a barrier between the Creator and that which He created. Anyone familiar with the Judean-Christian religion knows about the Trinity. It is not hard to see the immense wisdom of the Almighty who already at the beginning of time knew that this would all take place and that His Son and the Holy Spirit would combine to bring back to perfection those people that were chosen from the beginning of time, through the sacrifice of His Son after having become a human being in so far he became so physically, to break the barrier between God and man as indicated, that when He died, the temple curtain that was between the Holy and the Holiest of Holy was rend, indicating that now there was access again to God for the ones that Christ died for, because He became the high priest while, before, the high priest of the tribe of Levi only, was allowed to enter the Holiest of Holy to do the atoning work for the people with the blood of sacrificial animals, which was done once a year, for the forgiveness of sins, the people of Israel were guilty of committing. Christ became the High Priest Himself and through Him our sins are forgiven on a moment to moment basis, through prayer and supplications, instead of once a year. This is a deep study.

The fulfilling of the Law by Christ is what gives us our Salvation, our return to a state of perfection like when we first were created. Christ's blood washes away all sins. We become as an altar, which is, made a Holy vessel by the ceremonial sacrifice, on which Christ's blood is sprinkled as we become as one with Christ. We in essence become the body of Christ, putting on immortality not because anything we did, but because of God's grace and goodness toward mankind, not to let them live in darkness but live through and by the light given by His Son through the scriptures and through the called preachers of His word, who through the Holy Spirit, are able to translate the word in Spirit and in truth to those that are willing to hear, and to "activate" (in lieu of a better word) those who are called, according to God's plan because the called will recognize the sound of the Shepherd's voice through the preaching. The Bible states that many are called but few are chosen, were chosen, maybe a better-expressed way. We as human beings are hardly able to comprehend the great and unutterable honour of being chosen from all the people that are in the world and were in the world from the creation until now, because of our feeling of unworthiness even though we are made worthy by the blood of the Lamb (Christ). I'll say let us move forward in this life cautiously, knowing that unless our sins are forgiven us, we will have to give account for our actions and behaviour on judgment day. May God be merciful to us sinners and give His light to shine in our hearts so that we may see the road to salvation in all righteousness.

ABOUT MY COMPUTER

It's now about two months ago that I purchased a computer, the main reason being the price. My oldest son works in a electronics store and told me that if I wanted one, that the time was now on account he was getting a twenty percent discount at the Christmas holiday season plus since it was a floor model another twenty percent off on top of that. The offer was too tempting, so now I am the proud owner of a brand name computer that I have learned to call by its several names anywhere from "baby" to "jackass" because it would not do as I instructed. Needless to say that my proficiency in the use of my computer was less then a novice, however slowly but surely I am getting the hang of it and can perform the most basic set-ups on "the thing". My youngest son gets quite a kick out of it, by going on the Internet and uses it to get his college degree. His use of the computer seems almost effortless, you can see that his generation was weaned on pushbutton education. Yesterday he was doing a work assignment from school. He had started about nine in the evening and was still at it about one in the a.m. Finally with a sigh of relief, he was finished, as he reached over to press the print button he accidentally touched a keyboard key and to his consternation every thing got erased. You can well imagine the frustration and momentary anger at himself for being so careless and the computer that would not give him back his work. The thought came to me that a computer could be likened to a person and his or her relationship with the Creator and His son Jesus Christ the redeemer. For instance this, when I first got my computer I was told to get an anti virus program to prevent the computer from being invaded by program destroying viruses, this of course is computer language, those in the know understand what I am talking about. There seem to be a similarity between this and the parable of the sower who sowed wheat in a field and in the night the evil one came and sowed tares among the wheat, I compare the viruses with the tares that in the end will be destroyed. We as human beings store all kinds of information in our brain good and bad. The bad could be seen, as the virus started by Satan that invaded Adam and Eve and since then all of mankind became infested with this virus and we can see the results and the effect it has had on the human race, pain and suffering has been our lot.

I look upon the bible like a virus destroying program because in it is the way to get rid of all of our unrighteousness through Jesus Christ our Lord who is the great Eraser who can cleanse us from our contaminated programs through His blood. Hopefully I have in a small way made some of you aware of the similarities between the computer and us. A computer does not lie and is true to itself, it records faithfully what is stored in its memory banks. The same goes for a photograph it does not lie not even after many years it will always show the truth. These things are very close to being an absolute truth. About twenty years ago we where having a birthday party for my dad and everybody was having a good time and for a lark I put a tape recorder on the floor to record some of the goings on in the room. After about half an hour the tape ran out so I rewound it and started to play it back while the others were listening in, the recorder had picked up a conversation between two friends of my dad were one said something that was not very complimentary about somebody we knew and on hearing that, she immediately denied ever having said that. The truth sometimes hurt. Of course it had not been my intention embarrass anyone and I was kind of sorry about the whole affair, it was a spur of the moment thing but again the tape recorder did not lie and neither will our computer [brain] on judgement day

INNOCENT WORLD

A person's view on things on animate and also inanimate matters is always limited to what the mind has learned and experienced, up to the point of time that a particular situation comes up that needs to be evaluated and be judged upon, in order to sustain and maintain a relationship between it and the person doing the evaluating and judging. Limited knowledge will almost always result in poor judgment in a particular situation. Ergo, the greater a persons general knowledge, the more chance there is to have an accurate assessment of any given situation or point of view. There are very few people that do not have a point of view of creation and all the consequences involved therewith. There are however very few that have a true understanding of it all. It is hard to understand that at one time eons ago, there was nothing but empty space where now galaxies, are filling a tiny part of that indescribable void called "space." Galaxies upon galaxies with everyone having millions of stars; all having been created by the spoken word in an instant. The thoughts of the Creator instantly uttered, "by the Son in obedience to the Father," and brought into existence by the Holy Spirit and maintained by that Spirit until this day. This ever-creating Spirit having created the whole universe for the sole purpose of bringing into existence this world, we live in. Most people accept their existence as something that just happened to come about as time went by, not realizing that this tiny pinhead planet, compared to the universe is the only reason the entire universe was created. God knew from the beginning of time that there would be dissension among the angels that occupied heaven before the creation of the universe took place. The fallen angels being of a much higher order than "man" as we know them now, caused the earth to become a breeding ground and a battle ground of good and evil forces. We learn through the Bible that one-third of the angels were persuaded by Satan to follow Him, instead of God their Creator, as a consequence they have to be replaced by people who lived and those still living on this earth. These creatures have to be perfected or better said made perfect in all things in order to be ready to live in heaven.

RELIGIOUS THOUGHTS, STORIES AND POETRY

We all know that Satan caused Adam and Eve to lose their perfect status, by beguiling them and enticing them to disobey their Creator, by eating from the tree of the knowledge of good and evil and thus caused Adam and Eve and all their descendants to be damned and to be accursed because of their disobedience to God, all this because of Satan.

The creation itself is innocent, all the animals, insects, birds, fish, etc. are innocent in all this. The lion that catches and eats a few days old fawn is innocent in doing so, as it just follows it's instincts and cannot do other- wise as it would be against it's nature. In the Old Testament if an animal killed someone by kicking or any other means it had to die because it had spilled human blood. The same applied to a person that murdered another person, his blood had to be spilled and his life taken, it was a requirement instituted by God. If however a person caused another person to lose his life because of an accident or any other cause, including say, being kicked to death by a horse the other person owned, unless the horse was known to do this before time, then the person who owned the horse will have to compensate the bereaved family or forfeit his life, depending on the circumstances, but any other accidental death, the person causing it, had to compensate the family. In the world of nature actions done by animals are done innocently even though the strong will prey on the weak. The scorpion is innocent if it kills because it does what it does by nature and animals have not the ability to reason like man has. We through Adam are contaminated as we through him inherited his sin of disobedience and are a "fallen creature" unable to cleanse ourselves and were doomed to die in our sinful state without hope of eternal life, if it was not for Christ the saviour. The Creator in His wisdom has seen all this from the beginning of time and had a plan ready, like as to a rescue mission, by promising the Salvation of human kind, and sending His only begotten Son into the world at a set time, whom, all though innocent, He would suffer God's wrath of all of mankind because of mans disobedience. All sins of men, past, future and present, of people all ready dead, living and still to be born, whom where chosen from before the worlds were formed. All those sins were laid at His charge and He bore them in obedience to His Father, and the chosen ones "The Church" will be His. We speak of Heaven as a known place and we imagine all kinds of things about it. I perceive that it is a place where there is no discord, where serenity reigns and where the presence of the Father and the Son is that reward given in grace without us deserving it. A place where we are in a constant state of elation, like a person that won the lottery perhaps, or a person that scored the winning goal in a (from our standpoint) important game. It is a state of eternal bliss where the heart cannot help itself but to sing praises to the trinity that made it all possible.

WHAT ARE WE ANYWAY?

As mentioned in an earlier chapter, the senses of the human body are in the main, vision; taste, smell, hearing and feeling through the nerves in the skin and lets not forget the so called sixth sense which is perhaps that mysterious force that is a spiritual sense, unexplained, but still very much there, some call it a woman's intuition. I believe it to be a force that is part of creation, a built-in safe guard that often has been over looked by most people and depressed in others. It is probably the most active force left in man after the "fall" of human kind and is still used by the so called primitive tribes of the world. A normal person with all it's senses active, tends to think that he or she is master of his or her own destiny, this in my opinion this is far from true. I believe us to be like the universe itself or like the relationship between the sun and the earth and the earth and the moon. The interactions between planets is not of their own accord. The same as an atomic universe is not a free "something" but the atoms core holds the neutrons and the protons as well as the electrons in check by a field (electro-magnetic) that prevents the neutrons and protons to wander off somewhere. As a matter of fact, if it was not for this force, there would be nothing in existence because what is not held in check by some force, becomes nothing. So also it is with people, the interaction between them causes them to become what they are. The more is learned through interactions, the stronger the individual will become and could possibly become not unlike a solar system one being the sun, with others acting as planets in his or her solar system. Like a person starting his own company, the stronger willed and more intelligent the person is with a so-called vision, the more likely he or she is to succeed. At first in a small way with few people and later as time goes by possibly as big as ATT or General Motors that have become almost like super powers controlling the lives of thousands upon thousands of people. The person who started the company or firm may think that he has his or her own destiny in hand because after all here is this big company that he or she has started. He or she may not realize that the reason for the success is the interaction between himself and the people around him, whether it is the Vice-President or the person on the assembly line, so you see there is not much difference between these interactions and the interactions among the planets and stars or suns. What I really wanted to write about is the individual as a whole, what is he but a mass of atoms called body?

Of which the most important part is the brain, the nerve centre, through it, we may interpret every sensation we experience and therefore learn which is good which is bad and what is acceptable behaviour for interaction between individuals. The brain because of its nature tends to be self-serving. "Good Feelings" tends to please the brain, for what are a person but a brain with the ability to move from one place to another by use of his legs or any transportation available to the individual. Naturally, because of the make up of all the different people, whether by origin, nationality, race or religion whatever that person has learned or experienced, that is what he or she has become. Under normal circumstances a person never stops learning. The brain will never stop receiving and storing information learned or experienced on a daily basis or from second to second so to speak, we are not more then what we know. The reason that most people are self-serving is because the brain likes to be pleased through all the senses. Although our senses are mainly there for self-preservation and to warn us about dangers through taste, vision or touch or smell. At the same time the same senses give us pleasure through all kinds of applications, whether it be good food and drink, a pleasant aroma, a beautiful sight, sensual touching or just the feeling of well being. All these things are pleasing to the mind and all too often we overindulge through our senses. That is why in the religious world the brain has a tendency to stay shy of any kind of religion because ultimately it will put restrictions on the pleasure of the things we formerly enjoyed, only the need for something other than the physical will bring a person to the realization there is more to life than the enjoyment of the senses. There is however a feeling of an absence inside our heart, something missing and, unless the Creator Himself makes himself known to us, we will always have this empty feeling. The natural "man" will have nothing to do with it and although we know that we will not live forever and that there is an end to all things including ourselves, we are like lemmings going over a cliff into the cold ocean, because we follow the ones in front and cannot see the edge of the cliff until it is too late. I do not believe that there are many people who have not heard of heaven or hell, believing in it, is another matter. If a person comes to realize that there is a truth in that concept and he becomes worried about his state toward eternity, then he will be forced to inquire about things that are not of this world because the world as such cannot ease his mind about the spiritual things because there is no understanding of them, unless if be given to him from above, from a Higher Power. when this person comes to realize that the Creator of the Universe has an interest in him, not because he is special, but because from the beginning of time, some where chosen, it is said, "From before the worlds where formed." Imagine the honour to become the one picked out of the thousands upon thousands around us. The bible teaches us the whole story and purpose of creation. The reason for "man" to come into existence and the reason for God's Son Jesus to come on this earth is to conquer and overcome Satan and to set an example for the faithful to follow Him come what may, and to give His life for a ransom for many. Religion is a belief in things not seen, called faith, that He who has given the promises for this life as well as the next, can and will fulfill them in those that have this faith and the implant of Christ in them, through the born again experience. We must have faith and be faithful until the end of our life or until the rapture, in order to be counted worthy to receive eternal life. Amen.

OUR PURPOSE

A thought came into my mind about mankind on this earth. I could see that a person is given all those senses mostly for self-preservation in a sense, that if one was to detect smoke either through smell or sight he will instantly investigate the cause of it and put in safety himself and the people immediately around him. The same goes for sound, for the ear hearing the warning siren will put in safety the person that hears it. Then there is another sense like the inner self, it has also has the same sort of sense. Like a feeling of contentment after a wonderful meal or when someone tells us how beautiful we look or any other sort of flattery given. I suppose any kind of praise does the soul good in that it will give us a feeling of well being. We also would rather laugh than cry because laughing also will give us a feeling of "all is well with the world" and it is said laughing is good for the soul. A thing of beauty, to be admired whether it be a painting or a thoroughbred horse, it pleases the person's soul or inner being, so does a beautiful piece of music or the nice warm rays of the sun on the body after a cold winter or the taking of a warm bath, the good feeling after a hard fought game of tennis or any other sport and to have come out the winner. We seem to be forever occupied with our self, at least many of us do and do not see that our sole purpose on earth is to, strife for life eternal in the here after. Because we have also become to realize that there is also death eternal which is described as hell. We are like flowers in the field of life, that all of us live in and Gods word is as a butterfly going to and fro from flower to flower to find nectar and only those flowers that are not closed but are wide open and have nectar in them, will be visited by the butterfly. The nectar is the hope in the word that will set them free and implant in them the gift of eternal life. We have never lived in a time where it is so evident that the king of this world is Satan himself, we as a people are overwhelmed by it all and only those with very strong convictions will remain standing after the flood of evil that will come over the world, if it needs be that they remain, because the righteous will not see the destruction and desolation that has to come before Christ's return, but will be raptured and will return with Christ to the earth after the "Great Tribulation". Satan will be bound for a thousand years and will not be able to work his evil ways with anyone anymore. As I am nearing the end of our journey, I have become more and more aware that I have lived a foolish and unproductive life.

I have been an empty hollow sounding barrel of nothing, actually thinking at one time that I was something. I have been given, I believe the knowledge to see through everything and to discern the carnal and the spiritual things, but I am weak unto death and unless given the light in the heart and soul, it would have been a waste. But I do see and am waiting for God to give me for nothing, eternal life through His Son Jesus Christ. My thoughts are sometimes running rampant. To the "who's and why's" there is no end. I was thinking of the people that have gone before us, who are in the "now", where are they? Are they all in one place awaiting judgment together? Are the great mass murderers in the same place as the victims that they murdered and do the victims extract revenge on those who's victims they were (are), to these questions there also is no end. The mystery remains until we ourselves are called or unless this is revealed through the spirit of knowledge, suppositions are meaning less. Is the sweet old lady that lived down the street and recently passed away in the same place as Hitler or Genghis Khan? Can they all see the lake of fire? I suppose most people that believe in a here - after, fear death more then anything else in life unless they belong to the very few that are chosen from the foundation of the worlds to be with the Creator and His Son, the Son being their salvation, because they believed in Him and the work that He came on earth to do, namely this, that He laid down His kingly life for them and gave them the true insight of this event and it's purpose. I realize that these are only my opinions as I see them through the eyes of an ordinary human being.

THE BABY BIRDS

The day had started off cloudy but toward late morning the sun broke through the clouds and bathed everything with sunlight. It was early spring. May had just started and high in a maple tree a robin had build its nest with the help of her mate. The female robin had laid her eggs in the beautifully built nest, there were three of them and she had kept them warm for awhile now. It was all ready three weeks since she had laid the eggs and they were about to hatch. Father robin had kept a close eye on his mate to make sure that everything was all right and kept noisy neighbours at a distance by making threatening sounds by chirping loudly. Mother robin had heard a slight tapping sound coming from one of the eggs, she raised herself up to see and sure enough a small hole had formed in one of the eggs and she could see a small beak breaking through from the inside. Already she could hear small peeping sounds coming from the eggs. The birth of a baby chick was about to take place. She put her body back down on the eggs to make sure that a cold draft would not cool the hatching eggs down. Before the day was over, sure enough the eggs had hatched and three baby chicks lay snuggled up against the mother robin's warm chest. It was cozy in the nest and the chicks felt save and warm. The evening came and with it the dark and the quiet of the night. An occasional owl hoot could be heard and in the far distance the howl of some coyotes calling to the moon disturbed the silence of the night. But that too eventually stopped. Morning came all too soon. Already the chicks were stirring because they were hungry and they let their parents know by peeping loudly, as if to ask for food. Father robin had already left to find some juicy tidbits, like grasshoppers and insects, which the nestling would really enjoy. The chicks just could not get enough of them and father robin and soon also mother robin were busy flying back and forth to the nest with food for the chicks. About three weeks after the chicks had hatched they had grown quite a bit and were already as big as their parents, and were busily flapping their wings as if to fly away. But that would be still another week away. Sure enough five days later one of the chicks, was flying around, it happened actually by accident. He had been sitting on the edge of the nest flapping his wings when his little sister that also wanted to be on the edge of the nest accidentally pushed him off the nest.

It was a good thing that he had all his feathers because when he fell off the nest, he automatically spread his wings and to his amazement he began to fly and chirped with happiness. It was not long after, that his sister and other brother were also flying around. It made Mother and Father robin very proud.

It was a nice family that Robin family, wasn't it!

WHAT'S THIRTY YEARS

Yesterday my wife and I were married 30 years, it does not seem that long. I realize that most people that are together for this length of time say the same thing, "it does not seem that long" indicating that time is an elusive thing that can not be held in check but rolls on relentlessly, creating new things, situations and people to prove to us that there is very little in our hands. Everything is fitted together like a jigsaw puzzle, separate, the pieces are nothing, but together they form the whole picture and we are able to deduce from the picture what it is all about. As for this generation living in these times I truly believe that the times in store for this generation are of a sort that will make your hair stand on end. Blessed are those that see and prepare, so that these times don't come upon them, like a thief in the night as the "good book" says. I do not see any interest in religion in most kids. I do not believe that many of them pray before going to bed, to thank the good Lord for His blessings given that day and the kids do not get to know the way to salvation through bible reading, because it is withheld from them by the unbelieving parents, imagine the accusation of those kids in eternity against those parents and the terrible feeling of guilt and despair. May the good Lord prevent all this by coming into the heart of many a parent who sees, that without God, everyone is walking on quicksand and is liable to sink and who shall save them if there is no Saviour to grab their hand. I am thinking about the things eternal almost every hour of the day and I believe that God is working in me to make me see the way to salvation and eternal life, I know it and see it. May God through the Spirit make me comprehend it all?

THOUGHTS AND IDEAS

While going through my photo album, I looked into the past at those moments of time when the people in it were still alive and had thoughts and ideas and plans, loved and were loved. I was overcome with an incredible sadness, and my heart went out to those people that are not with us and my mind and heart tried to breach the gap between the now and the past. Knowing the futility of it, my mind refused to let go, but all that came to the fore were the memories and I guess it has to suffice since there is no other way to enter into the past than, through memories. Of course the wish is that it wasn't so and at times we wouldn't mind going into the past to do or undo things we did or did not do. Would it not be something if we could go back into the past and say to someone you knew that you cared about him or her and to ask for a hug or kiss or both, to say a last good-bye? But like I said wishing does not make it so. Sometimes in our dreams we relive the past and it seems as real as reality until we wake up, alas it was a dream.

It seems to me that we have very little reality if one comes to think of it. Time does not stop. No, not for a moment. The seconds even divided into mille-seconds don't make time stand still. Ergo we are creatures of the past, every object we look at be a chair next to you or a hill miles away or a star, light years away. We look into the past because it takes time for any visual contact to reach our eye and for the brain to interpret what we are looking at. Sound is even slower than the speed of vision or light. Anyone that ever has seen a person chop or split wood a fair distance away, will tell you that the sound of the axe striking the wood, lags far behind the speed of vision. But enough already before reality becomes so real and we talk or write ourselves out of existence. Talking about existence, I guess it can only be proven through our relationship with our environment and its surroundings. Did we have a pre-existence and was the Spirit that is now in us, in another realm with the Creator? He that knows all things knows this too. It is not really important to know this because the now is here and the story about mankind as explained in the King James version of the

RELIGIOUS THOUGHTS, STORIES AND POETRY

Old and New Testament makes hardly any mention of these things, although in some instances a pre-destined or pre-ordained happening is indicated for some people before they are even born. I imagine that a lot of people are disturbed for instance about the fact that God says in His word, that He loved Jacob but hated Esau and that, before they were born.

It is not difficult to deduce from this that God already had seen the end result of both lives, this not only explains that some people, have found favour with God but also that the election already took place before the worlds were formed and that time just passes until the time is full or runs out like sand out of an hour glass. Most people get hung up on time, not realizing that time only exists for our sake and that by God there is no time, only present and when God said that He loved Jacob and hated Esau, He already had seen the end of Esau's and Jacob's life and Esau did with his life which was not to Gods honour.

When I think about perfection, I believe a circle to be a symbol of perfection, there is no beginning and no end and I compare it to the universe as there is nothing in the universe that does not rotate one way or another and has a generally round shape, anywhere from the smallest atom to the most distant galaxy. The making of the universe had only one purpose, to create man or Adam, because the all knowing creator, he who is called the Alpha and the Omega; the beginning and the end, the One who no one is allowed to question, the "I shall be what I shall be!" knew that Satan, that angel of light. Who was over the heavenly musicians and the musical instruments, would become a fallen angel who would draw away 1/3 of the heavenly creatures. Ergo the creation was solely for this reason, to replace those fallen angels with the elect, at such time when the last Born Again Christian will be gathered unto him. Then the purpose of creation will be fulfilled and the lamb that was slain from the foundation of the world will claim His people that believed in Him and who's sins are forgiven through Christ's saving work. Amen.

THE BRAIN

To make an analysis of oneself seems on the whole an elusive thing. For what are we? What is our being? Although we have a physical presence, are we what we show in that presence or are we more then that? Are we a spiritual being which shows itself through the physical form we have attained? Becoming an adult, what represents us, our smile or the way we look? How do others perceive us? What is it about us for instance that makes us attracted to or by the opposite sex? Do we emit a scent from our glands that either attracts or repels others and what are the needs of this physical form that has the ability to use it's brain to manipulate, help or elate others? We know for a fact that if the brain is not stimulated in the early years of childhood, that child will lag behind in understanding and knowledge of the world around him or her. It is not hard to figure out that we are in essence what our brain contains. The good things learned, the "bad" and the indifference of it all. Basically in our relationships with other human beings we like to hear nice things about ourselves and criticism is a thing we hate with a passion unless we have learned through self-analysis that there are certain areas in our being that could stand some improvement. Ergo, a certain amount of criticism is good in a sense that we improve on our self-image and the way others see us. If someone flatters us we seem to take a liking to that person after all he pleased our senses and makes us walk on air through his or her flattery. The brain always seems to need this. Like watching a good movie or seeing beautiful scenery, having a wonderful relationship, good food, drink or anything that pleases any of our six senses and therefore the core of our being, is the brain.

GOD THE FATHER
RIGHTEOUS AND TRUE
GOD THE SON
THE REDEEMER
GOD THE HOLY SPIRIT,
OUR HELPER

God's standard of perfection **THE LAW**   OT NT The scriptures to
give us light on the way to our salvation
MAN

with his rebellious nature

God's ways are not man's ways and who can fathom the mind of the
Creator. I suppose many an attempt has been made, but only the
redeemed through Christ's sacrifice are able to give some account
of what God is because Christ has made it known to them. To me God is
life and a life giving entity. All through nature is this visible, from the
smallest living organism to the tallest tree; life is inborn and sustained
through God's laws of nature by the Holy Spirit. There is no plant or tree
that does not bring forth seeds, to assure it continues the species. The same
goes for the animal world and all other living things including bacteria
or the smallest of insects. Cells are formed constantly to replace the one's
that died or to give growth to whatever it is that is being formed. I stand
in awe to see it all come to pass. We plant a seed from a flower and sure
enough, with proper care such as the right soil, moisture etc. a wondrous
thing happens. The seed undergoes a transformation (some say it dies) and

it starts roots to feed itself and to obtain moisture while at the same time striving to grow out of the darkness into the sun-light to obtain growth (through photo synthesis) and to become the flower so designated as the DNA in the seed dictates. The wisdom of Solomon was but a piece of dust on a weighing scale (to paraphrase David his father) compared to God's wisdom.

We as mankind will never be able to understand but little if anything of God's wisdom, power, majesty and His love towards mankind. We are not unlike plants or trees. We too have the ability to procreate. Plants and trees being immobile, need either the wind to carry the spores or insects such as bees or birds to secure the continuation of their kind, while we as human beings are able to come together voluntarily to secure a continuation of our species, God willing. There are so many thoughts entering my mind that I cannot keep up, from the election of certain people out of the centuries past and the future, up to the time of the great tribulation. There is a wonderful story in the N.T. in which Jesus likens the human race as to a field in which seeds are strewn, the seed being the word and this is what this piece of writing is all about on account God Himself also wants to grow and expand through the spirit coming into the hearts and minds of them that from the beginning of time were selected or elected through God's grace and wisdom, from every generation, from Abel until now. That is why we are duel creatures that have a corruptible body but an eternal Spirit. I truly believe that the only reason for the creation of everything including the universe itself is to give to mankind the ability to procreate so that the Creator could gather His chosen ones through the centuries from the procreated and until such time when the last chosen ones are gathered together that will come out of the great tribulation via the rapture before and during, to be with Christ their Lord and Saviour, until He will come again, touching down on the mount of Olives. Then Satan will be bound for a thousand years until the time is fulfilled for that great judgment, after Satan is come out of the bottomless pit to do his evil deeds for a short season. Needless to say that there will be great sorrows and whether there will be survivors after the great tribulation I don't really know and whether the people at the end of the thousand years, whom Satan, after he is loosed out of the bottomless pit will beguile, are descendants of the righteous that came with Christ. I don't know and probably should research it more. However these are my thoughts and interpretations. It seems that for every answer we think we have, there are many more questions that only will be answered when we reach perfection through Jesus Christ our Lord.

MY THOUGHTS ON THE SUBJECT OF LOVE

When first thought of, it seems a very easy thing to explain what love is. However now that I have sat down and started to think about it, it seems somewhat elusive, because it is not something that you can take a hold of in a manner of speaking and show it to others while holding it up for everyone to see. Only in the expressions by words, touch or other actions, it seems to express itself. All romance books are about love and all the diverse writers are telling their readers what they think love is and what it does once it goes in motion. I believe that true love is an exceptional thing rather than the rule. The good book puts it in a better way than any other book in my view, when it says that no person has more love than he or she who would lay down his or her life to save another. This is a truism that very few can deny. I realize that love has many forms and is sometimes interpreted wrongly in a sense that lust is mistaken for love or liking something, this of course does not constitute love although I can see a relationship between love and liking, but when one does dissect both, the differences become apparent. I think that love is the most unselfish emotion that one can experience. Love does not tire nor condemn anyone. It is kind and understanding and knows no hate (which is the evil side of a deep emotion). Love does not serve self first. True love will never die. I believe that a loving person will not get drunk or become violent, say things that will hurt others or do them. He or she may have done all these things at one time or another, but once true love enters one's heart and mind, these things that were before, will now become a thing of the past, never to return. I believe true love is not unlike a born again experience. The silver cord will keep the connection even after death, with the Trinity granting us eternal life through faith and love for Him who died so we may live.

MY THOUGHTS ON BATTLEGROUND

In the garden of the idealist there are no weeds. This sort of statement could get a person making it, into hot water, but its fair to say that it is not too far from the truth. I guess an idealist constantly battles the ignorance of other people who don't know what an idealist really is. He constantly seeks perfection in all things, whether it is in his surroundings or in his or her relationships with other people or in the things he or she does for a living. They are "ideal" workers to have on one's staff. Unfortunately in an imperfect world to achieve an ideal that is perfect is virtually impossible since only the Creator is perfect and whatever "emits" (for lack of a better word) from the Creator is perfect, forever changing but always remaining the same. So the idealist has a battlefield of his own making. There are other battlefields, as a matter of fact there are thousands of them and to bring them up to make readers aware of them would take a lifetime. We all have our own battles to fight. The farmer, for instance, has to fight invasions of bugs, fungi etc. or an illness in his animals. He fights them by spraying his fields with insect repellent and inoculating his cattle against various diseases, while a gardener constantly fights weeds and insects of all kinds in his garden. A working man battles traffic, disagreements with his boss or co-workers etc. and then there are the battles of the impaired or physically handicapped and the mentally disabled, people that have had strokes, heart attack survivors and people that have gone through an operation. Then there are those who have lost a loved one who are battling to overcome that loss and in later years battle the loneliness that follows. So you see that there are many battles, each different to a certain extent from the other. And then my thoughts go out to the battles of people during an argument or on a larger scale between families, taking for instance the McCoy's and the Hatfield's and then the armed conflicts between nations and in our time the wars between east and west. There is very little middle ground anymore; you are either for or against. The insanity of it all. A person does not have to be religious to see that egotism is the devil's food, that one up-man-ship that thrives in our society, sports and games being the main culprit, better than you or "holier than thou" is first and foremost in people's thoughts most of the time and they don't see that they are dying and that the short life span given to us as human beings is better spent loving one another.

Unfortunately the ruler of this earthy realm will have none of that, ever since Adam went against the Creator and so gave up to Satan this jewel in the universe, this earth, this creation by the Almighty. It wasn't long before Satan's influence was felt, when Cain slew his brother Abel and it has not changed much since then. When my thoughts enter the battlefields of war between nations and I see the millions of young men dying in the strength of their lives, the cries for a loved one on their lips while staring eternity in the face, the hurt showing on their faces and then the dawning of the realization that the end is there, no more laughs, no more merriment with the fellow soldiers, no more caresses with the one you love, no more anything, what a heart rending scenario, repeated over and over from Abel until now. Every day over one hundred and fifty thousand people die from every cause. It's hard to believe that one day we also will be one of these, nevertheless it is our fate. The times we live in have been foretold by the seers from the past, also the coming of Christ, and those that are found in Him will be raptured (taken up) before the "Great Tribulation" such as never was nor ever will be on earth.

THOUGHTS ABOUT ME

Where this urge to write constantly comes from I cannot tell you, only that it is there. The thought occurred to me to evaluate myself, honestly without being biased. Since I am inside myself I may honestly assume that I know myself best. I realize that others may see me in a different light because of past experiences and dealings with me and the memories of that could make it possible that the assessment of myself is not the same as others see me. It's true that one's character is formed during the early years of one's existence. It's also true that the mother more or less raises the children since the father goes out to earn a living and is mostly only around in the evening hours and therefore only sees the children a few hours a day, except on weekends. If the father is in shift work it becomes a different matter altogether, because the father needs sleep in the morning because he only came home at three thirty that morning, the children therefore have to be kept quiet, which, especially if there is an rambunctious child, could build a sort of resentment towards the father in the child's early years, I just want to point out the possibility of this I thought I put that in. As far as my character is concerned, I will start off with this - what and who am I? Now that I am at this point and try to get a hold of myself so to speak, I find myself very elusive and hard to pin down because we as human beings tend to put our best foot forward and forget about our "bad" traits. I know for a fact that at times I am short tempered which is not at very pleasant thing to be especially if one is on the receiving end. So that must be called a negative trait. Quite often I have been told and also IQ tests have proven that I am a person with a little above average intelligence. It makes me wonder on account of the really dumb things I sometimes do. There is a tendency to be vindictive, but not overly so. I have no hatred towards anyone although I may hate what they do or say if untrue or totally unfounded. Having been brought up by Christian parents I have adopted that religion for my own and have tried to pass this on to my own children. I must admit that it was a dismal failure on my part to accomplish this. My wife has never taken a real active part, by for instance, reading the bible at mealtimes in my absence, but she did teach them to say their evening prayers before bedtime.

Religion is in my every day thoughts and will be until I die or if I am found worthy to be raptured before Christ's coming before the "Great Tribulation". One of my better traits is that I can be counted on. I have no malice towards anyone, am easy to get along with unless antagonized by others through word or deed, that are untrue or detrimental towards the family as a whole or to me personally. I love games that need brainpower to solve or need a general knowledge such as crossword puzzles. Checkers is my favourite with chess being a close second. I am good at playing card games of any kind and seem to have the uncanny ability to see things coming on before they happen. I know that this involves what is generally known as ESP, but how it works I don't know. As a young man I knew for instance that one-day I would be blessed. This has now happened with God's help and permissiveness. May we be benevolent towards others that are less fortunate, because being rich could become a curse to those who won't share their wealth. I always was quite athletic and some of it is still there but at an age of almost sixty-two it is fast disappearing. I believe myself to be a person with a sense of humour but am generally a serious one. I like for everything to be in its place and a place for everything and can become quite upset if others upset my apple cart by using and abusing and not putting things back where they got them from. One could say that this is petty and come to think of it I am petty, too much so and am liable to lash out in anger because of it. I like to think I am a good communicator although not so much in front of a crowd but would like to practice that some time. I am a light sleeper and wake up easily if even a slight noise is made in the immediate area. It is possible that this could be the cause of my sometimes short temper. I am fairly generous but could use some improvements on that. I like to see things grow, especially what I have personally planted and I enjoy nature itself with its wonders immensely. I enjoy fixing things and like to see and read things from the past and have a tendency to live in the past. I guess one could say that I raised my children fairly strict and may not have given them enough breathing space which also caused my children to have a certain resentment against me and understandably so, my dad raised me that way, so I did not know any other way although I was a lot more lenient than my dad ever was. It is therefore possible that my children see me as a sort of tyrant that restricted them in their "enjoyment" of life because of their dad's religious beliefs that would not permit them to have their way.

I myself went through this stage, not realizing or comprehending the necessity of the father in any religious family, to pass on to their children the way of salvation through Jesus Christ our Lord. Failing to do so would result in eternal damnation through the very act of withholding "the way" from their children. Without the reading of "the Word of God" (the Bible) this is impossible, because by not reading the bible to one's children, even the possibility of salvation is vanished and in their hereafter the children we raised will curse us until all eternity, how lovingly the relationship may have been on earth. I will not go into our sexual behaviour except to say that male and female have a tendency to become sexually perverted on a moment's notice and to deny this is folly. It is the persistence in this tendency that makes for an unhealthy relationship, enough already. There are very few people who don't know in their heart the wrong doings of such actions and are condemned in their own mind by their consciences. There is no doubt that I could be called lazy but not all the time. When I get my teeth into something it will come to a successful conclusion ninety nine percent of the time. I am always willing to help others even if it is to my own detriment and really don't expect anything in return besides a thank you very much. That is usual enough gratification for me. I feel sometimes that people at times, are taking full advantage of me without realizing that they do. It seemed to be a normal thing for them almost like Barnum and Bailey pointed out at one time, "there is a sucker born every minute." I guess it is like the young birds in a nest that open their beaks wide and expect the parent bird to feed them, except these are older birds.

A PSALM OR TWO

My cry goes out to my God who lives
For to whom will I go to, there is no one
That understands and knows my heart
All the day long my thoughts go out to thee
Come hastily my God and maker of my soul
For I am in derision and why should I go down
Into that realm where darkness reigns
Save my soul alive from the clutches of Satan
And lead me in thy ways and make my minds eye
To see that which would make me walk the path
Of righteousness and truth however stumblingly
Pull me and bring me into the presence of thy Son

That He may take away this burden from my heart
And mind, this barrier between me and thee
Then will my soul lift itself up out of the mud
And praise thy name for all eternity.
Where was I when thou created the worlds?
Was I with thee and didst thou thrust me out?
Was I in thy bosom and didst thou love me then?
Why hast thou cast me out so that I dwell here?
My eternal soul calls to thee to restore me
As I was then when I dwelled among the stars
When I was innocent, lovely and kind
Now I wear these dirty rags and sin is my portion
I am black and am not able to cleanse myself
The mire of this earth cleaves onto me
There is no love no compassion no understanding
In me, my Lord come and cleanse me from this
Poison that has saturated my soul and mind
Be merciful unto me and grant me this my wish
Because why should I go down into the bowels
Of the Earth where this blackness is king
Lord let thy son also have died for me, this worm
That I am, then shall my heart lift itself up
And my eyes shall see the morning star that herald
My place in eternity that I may be with thee again.

THOUGHTS ABOUT ME

"DREAM ON"

The early light of dawn breaks through
When I still sleep and dream of you
Reality it seems so far away
The world of work, the world of play
Are far removed from what I dream
Although the dawns first light does gleam.

"MAY I HAVE THIS DANCE"

The music's soft, the lights are low
We dance to it, with love aglow
Within our hearts that now are one
It's destiny that has us drawn
Together until death us part
That is a sign of a true heart.

"THE RAIN"

The rain falls softly to the ground
It makes things wet that's all around
Giving drink to grass and tree
And freshen up it seems to me
The world around us and I am glad
The Angels are not really sad.

"TIMELESSNESS"

The waves roll in like runners to the shore
In endless rows they come forever more
When long I am gone they're coming still
The shore will never get it's fill
The rivers flow into the ocean wide
But even so the waters will abide
Within the borders set of old
In summer warm in winter cold.

IT'S ONLY SEASONA

A cold wind blows through the naked tree
Snow's all around us as far as the eye can see
This lonely tree does touch my heart
It really does until I start
To think about the spring that brings about
A change in nature all throughout
This tree will be clothed again with leaves
And so will all the other trees.

OUR GOAL

Our goal in life must ever be
Alike as to the apple tree
To bring forth fruit for everyone
Then can we say that we have done
What the Creator of us did ask
And have fulfilled our earthly task.

THOUGHTS ABOUT ME

FATHER TIME

Although we see, we don't perceive
Youth will be taken by a thief
The thief's disguise is Father Time
All youth he takes yes even mine.

NATURE

A coyote howls in the night so still
I also hear the whippoorwill
They cry to make their presence known
And make the area their own
A place to keep the others out
It's what nature is all about.

BUSINESS OPPORTUNITY

A plum a plum I see a plum
I grab a hold with finger and thumb
O boy o boy it's now I see
I got hold of a bumblebee.

NEAR AND FAR

Even though I am far away
I think of home ne'er every day
Of things I did and didn't do
The happy times the sad times too
I know the past I cannot alter
The more I try the more I falter
What's done is done it seems to me
Change what you can the rest let be.

ABIDE

It's yonder hill that beckons me
From there it is that I can see
The other world that's not my own
But alien to what I've known
My world, it is not built with stone
But just a farm where I have grown
And learned to live a simple life
A world that is not full of strife
So here it is I will abide
And not cross to the other side
Where cities thrive and have their ways
My home I love, no other place.

A MOTHER'S LOVE

Behave yourself my mother said
Or I will send you to your bed
I better heed my mother's words
Before she will be out of sorts
I love my Mom and she loves me
That's plain for everyone to see
She hugs me close when I am cold
Cause after all I am four years old

"PERSEVERE"

Our dreams will sometimes turn to dust
However going on we must
To build new dreams that will last longer
Adversity will make us stronger
Don't hang your head and pine away
Tomorrow is a brand new day.

AWARENESS

The Creator's work is passed understanding
His miracles are never ending
From planets, stars and grass so green
I fear that no one has ever seen
The hand of God in everything
However praise to Him we sing
His hands reach out to us all
Please let us listen to his call
Eternity that's what's at stake
Don't fall asleep but stay awake
Prepare yourselves with open hearts
So that your soul when it departs
Shall find a home where love will reign
Where hate and lies are alien.

GOOD AND EVIL

There is a subject in this world that involves us all, not only as a nation, with all it's different ethnic groups, religious domination creeds of all kind, but also as individuals, which is the matter of good and evil. We don't have to be saints, intellectuals, young or old to know this. We all have good and bad traits in us and the ability to carry these out. Because the word good comes before bad. I would like to put on paper what I believe to be something that is good. "Is good a force of some kind?" I believe this to be so; the same is true for bad or evil forces. Make no mistake this earth of ours is a battleground, between the two and the souls of the inhabitants of the world is the prize between them. To be "good," as far as one could be "good", one has to be kind, gentle, loving, caring, patient, not prone to anger, strong drink or have an overindulgence of any kind, quick to forgive if wronged, help out where help is needed, give to the poor and donate time or money to any charitable organization, obey the law of the land you live in and the persons in authority. I realize that all this is hard stuff for most of us and almost impossible to abide by, because who wants to be a "goody, goody." Still it is the way the Creator had intended for it to be. But the evil one from whom sprung all that was bad and contrary to good, interfered with it and caused Adam and Eve to believe him, instead of their Creator and therefore, brought all the calamities that subsequently followed into this world that was created in perfection and was the cause of the first war between two people, Cain and Abel and we know the result of that war. It has been like that ever since. I don't think I have to explain to anyone what bad or evil is; it is the opposite of all things good mentioned. There will always be men like the Caesars of old or Attila the Hun, Alexander the Great, Stalin, Hitler, Mussolini, Napoleon and all the Kings of old who conquered other Kings, and tried to carve out an empire for themselves. They imposed their will on others to do their bidding, bringing untold grief through death and destruction upon others. I don't think these people ever sat down and wondered about a hereafter and the consequences of their actions and if they did, may have found it to be in accordance with the thinking of the times. They will have their reward.

The Greek Philosophers did try to bring a peaceful solution to it all by exporting their philosophy to other nations, but Alexander the Great took things in his own hands and exported Greek Philosophy by force, even if he may not have intended to do so. The odd thing about it all is that the way to a peaceful co-existence between peoples and nations was there. Given by the Creator to His oracle people whose patriarch was Abraham. From whom the Israelites find their origin, their writings which became the "Torah" from which we have our Old Testament with the New Testament, being incorporated into what we know now as our bible after Christ's life on earth, which his disciples recorded. There are probably very few people that never have heard of the bible in today's world, where new information can reach any point on earth within seconds, although I would imagine there are some people that live in isolation from the rest of us and then there are some Countries that have banned the book through government, believing it to be a danger to the way of life imposed upon those people, calling the bible subversive. Religions, like Buddhism, Hindu, Muslim and the like have their own writings and teachings. But lack what I consider a very important aspect and that is the fact that only the bible has in it, that God also loved the world that He sent to this world his only begotten son Jesus, to tell and teach the world what God was and what was expected from mankind, if the people wanted to obtain eternal life via Christ's teachings and through the sacrifice of his own life. This is a great mystery and only those to whom God will reveal this through the Holy Spirit, are able to understand the secrets of creation to the passing away of it all. Let us therefore listen to the small voice within our hearts that begs us to consider our pathway on which we walk in this life. Because our soul knows and longs for freedom of damnation.

ABOUT LOVE

Not long ago I remembered inadvertently a line from a song that went like this; "What Is This Thing Called Love?" Personally I would not call it a thing, because it is an emotion that can have a profound effect on us if we are perceptive to it and can form a lifetime bond between people and people or between people and pets. A person could love a painting or a car or any other inanimate object, but that object cannot return the love or admiration you have for it. Therefore it is a one sided emotion. Love for an animal is very different because it will react to the way you treat it. A dog will wag it's tail for instance, while a cat will start to purr to indicate that it cares for the friendly manner you treat it. Of course animals in the wild, will care for their own kind and show quite affection for their young under ordinary circumstances. I would presume this behaviour to fall under animal instinct and not love, as we know it. Love will come in all different forms, although from the same source. For instance "Puppy Love" can be quite passionate but will shortly fade away in most cases. Then there is an infatuation with another person. I guess one could call that a mild form of love which could grow of course into a "full blown love." Then there is "Lust," which is often mistaken for love and usually turns out to be a very selfish thing that can be mutual between people and I suppose does satisfy a need to be loved by another person. Then there is the unreturned love, or the one-sided love that one can have for someone who is totally unaware of it and thinks that you are just being friendly. I realize that there are loves that are not natural, as we know them in the realm of religion and are frowned upon. Personally I don't see anything wrong with a man loving another man or a woman loving another woman. But because love between people is usually expressed (between a man and a woman) through the sex act, I would put it to the reader that sex acts between people of the same gender is unnatural, because the Creator created man and woman and for those two to become one flesh through the sex act and to become pro-creators with the Creator himself. Needless to say that this is impossible between two people of the same gender, therefore, I must come to the conclusion that God never meant this to be that way. Let me assure you that I will never impose my will upon anyone in regards to these matters. But I would like to express my point of view and hope that I could possibly enlighten some people that are in such relationships because eternity awaits us all.

Then there is love that can be like a lightning strike between two people that meet purely by chance, that instantly knowing that something very special just happened. And if both people are free to pursue their relationship, love will blossom like a flower that is changing from bud to full blossom and they will be oblivious of anything or any people around them. It's a beautiful thing to see if one has an eye for it. Then there is the love between family members, which is the most important love of all. Because if love is withheld, a family could die as a family because of it. And hatred between them could flare up, with all it's grief and sorrows. May the good Lord give wisdom to all parents to raise their family with love and respect for each other. Lastly, I would like to say this about love. Love is not selfish. It is given without hesitation, without expectation. It is not I love you, if you love me. Far from it! It's more I love you because you are, no return necessary, it is given without reservations. While writing this I see my own shortcomings in all of this and the limits I have put on my own giving of love and affection towards my family and friends, proving that deeds do count and not words. Then there is the love that someone has for another, that he or she would lay down their life in order to save the person they love. That sort of love is of a pureness that only our Father in heaven can give. Like He gave his only begotten son for a ransom for many. Weep for those that consider this lightly, their sorrows will be manifold.

ABOUT BELIEF

How often don't we hear the expression; "I have faith in you." As to the ability to do or to abstain from doing a certain thing. We all know that the word "faith" is used mostly in the realm of religion and usually in the same breath as belief or believe. These three words are often used in interaction with one another. Like, "I believe in my belief," or "I have faith in my faith." There are obviously numerous applications of these words and not always in religious matters. Most people think that belief and faith are pretty well the same thing. I for one don't think so and not because I am from Missouri, "the show me state." I believe that a certain belief is a set of tenets or rules to be followed, that then places you into this group of believers, when accepted by them, which in turn causes a person to become a Roman Catholic, Presbyterian, Muslim or whatever this group makes itself out to be and it becomes his or her faith. It seems straightforward enough, however, I believe faith to be something more substantial. Faith is a firm belief in something that's unseen and unverifiable. I guess the expression "blind faith" is about as close as one could get to this explanation. In the religious world or realm, (myself being of the Judean-Christian faith), this faith that we are talking about can only be given in our hearts by our Creator through the Holy Spirit. It can not be learned or taken on by ceremonies of one kind or another. It is a gift from the Almighty, to the ones chosen from before the worlds were formed. Needless to say that it is a great honour bestowed upon that person that has been given the third eye to be able to discern the physical from the spiritual and to understand creation and the reason for it. To be able to live his or her life in accordance to the scriptures given to mankind. To prepare him or her for the here after. That's why Bible reading is an essential and absolute necessity for our children as well as ourselves, if we are to understand and able to open our hearts to the outpouring of the Holy Spirit.

PASSING TIME

It seems such a short time ago that I was walking through the melting snow, when the temperature reached an unprecedented height of 4° above zero C°, that April day in 1997. I remember the chickadees putting up a fuss in the surrounding trees, no doubt they were heralding the coming of spring, with much more vigour than I thought necessary. But what do I know? I too looked forward to the warmer weather that was on its way. It seems as one gets older the winter months seem to take forever to pass by and the cold starts to affect the bone structure and is causing a stiffness among the moving parts of the body. Most of us who are in their fifties and sixties can verify this. Finally as spring was approaching, the flower beds and garden plots were being prepared and after the 24th of May weekend, it was safe to start planting our favourite plants and flowers in the flower beds, while the garden was being filled with all the assorted veggies that we liked to eat, nothing like home grown you know. By now most of the trees had their adornment in the form of leaves because "who wants to look at a naked tree anyway?" Before long, the grass needed cutting and before we knew it summer was in full swing. The rain did not fall in an over abundance in the early summer and the thought of crop failure in our area was the talk of the day among the farmers. But just as everything looked really bad, the rains came and eased the fear of many a farmer. Now it is already October 10 and the wind is howling around the corners of the house and the temperature is in the high fifties and the promise of winter is in the air. The leaves are coming off the trees by the millions, as they cannot withstand gusts of wind coming in from the north, the lawn is full of leaves and once in a while a swirling wind picks up the leaves like a mini tornado and deposits them in the field adjacent to our property. A kind of sadness comes over me seeing all this happening and I become so aware of the passing of time and the inability to hold on to it. I thank my God that all this is only the preparation for the coming of spring, six months from now and we again will rejoice in the coming of a season that pleases us to no end.

THOUGHTS ON TRUE

As I was sitting at the dining room table, I began to think about what the word true actually means. I suppose that it has many similarities with the word truth, because if a person were to say, King so and so of England, died say in 1684, we assume that he is telling the truth and if we were to go into the history books to research this statement we may find, that this event actually took place in 1684. So we must accept it as the truth, but this truth is very general and not really a true statement as no particulars are given, for instance, "what day was it?" did this King die in the morning, afternoon, evening or during the night, and even if we did find this out, at what hour and after we found that out, what minute? And then what second and then what milli-second etc. After that we may want to determine what the cause of his death was? What part of the body was affected and after that we can go into the body to find the exact cause and then go back to find the cause of the cause. As you can see it is an endless futile circle as to find the truth and what is true, on account of truth and true being so generally accepted for what they represent imprecise and general. I realize that we as human beings don't need the precise truth to go on in life, because there are very few absolute truths. I heard someone say one time that the only thing on this earth, and I suppose in the universe, that remains the same, is change, now there is a deep thought. I take this to be one of the absolute truths. To say for instance that spring will come seven months from now, this being September, will only be true if the changes that always take place are not too drastic, but this statement as such is no absolute truth. Then the possibility exists that even if spring where to come at the said time, but all the people on the earth had perished, there won't be anyone to verify this event, as the trees don't speak to each other, so what is truth and what is true? It is something very elusive when looked at below the surface. As you can see anything and everything can be philosophized about and made to disappear into nothingness. I guess this is a try at futility and it almost worked.

WHO ARE YOU

Our thoughts, they come and go like waves in the ocean. Some remain awhile, but then, like most thoughts they pass into oblivion, never to be renewed. Some however, seem to return at their own volition over and over again until they, if it were possible would drive us into insanity or provoke us to commit an insane act. I guess they would fall under the category murderous thoughts and the more quickly we disperse with those, the better for us, as they are from the dark side of our inner self. If we do let these forces take a foothold it would not be long before the acting out of them would start. Anyone who has sat down and contemplated his or her purpose of being and has crawled inside him or herself trying to find the core of their being, probably came away disappointed as there is nothing of which it can be said, "here it is" and holding it up for everyone to see almost like a trophy, after all you have found yourself and here it is.

I believe the "self" to be in constant change. As the circumstances surrounding us change, so does our "self" or our personality." We can not be more than what we have learned or experienced in life and we are molded so to speak into a person, by race, religion, environment and friends, but most of all by our parents. The parents are in the end responsible for the children's upbringing and their early childhood education. As I look back to the time that our three children were growing up, I can see the mistakes made, knowing what I know now, "it's water under the bridge" as my mom would say. All the too's are generally not good in bringing up a child as in too lenient or too strict etc. It is generally accepted that a spoiled child is usually void of any feeling for others, it is a result of the upbringing. A child that has been taught to share things, is more likely to be able to get along with their peers in harmony, than the ones not taught this basically sound principle. Spoiled children have a tendency to be without much self-discipline and are much easier drawn into a world of drug users and are more likely to become involved with crime. On the other hand a child that was loved too much by the parents and protected from all the so called "evil influences" is more likely to get hurt once he or she is released, (if that's the right word), into society with all it's violence and attractions that a person like that is suddenly exposed to. It's obvious that there has to be a happy medium as they say.

The children that are well adjusted, have most likely wise and caring parents, that did not spare the rod when necessary, because they did it out of love and were always there when the child needed them for anything at all. It is a sad thing to see all the marital break-ups and the position it puts the children in especially when they are of a tender age. For them to become well adjusted adults is very hard for the single parent to accomplish, since he or she is most likely a working stiff who has to support this family, and time spent with the family is restricted to the evening hours and weekends, while of old it is said that raising children is a full time job. There are a lot of parents that don't believe in disciplining a child for a misdeed of one kind or another because they are afraid that the child would start to hate them for it. I believe this to be a misconception. Naturally by disciplining a child I don't mean to beat the child within an inch of it's life, but just enough to cause a slight discomfort that will register in the brain and store it and associate the act with the discomfort it brought about and therefore in future abstain from doing it again, wilfully. In nature among the apes for instance, a youngster that becomes too boisterous will be slapped around so to speak, by a senior member of the troupe to keep it in line. The same happens in a lion tribe with youngsters that are a little too wild, they get stiff-armed by the adults to calm them down. It is surprising how we remember events associated with pain involved. Physical pain that is, we may forget many events that have taken place in our lives but events involving pain are instantly recalled. Raising children is a very difficult job, but the rewards could be more then ever expected for those that do it wisely and lovingly. Always remember we don't own our children, we just borrow them from our Creator and their destiny is eternity.

ABOUT FALL AND US

Here I am sitting at the dining room table looking out on the distant hills and look upon the trees in all their fall splendor, there are maples, aspen, birch and walnut, and stands of pine trees that really show up very green among the trees whose leafs are turning, as they say. The colours are already variant from soft bronze to bright red and very pleasing to the eye. It is an unusually mild day for the time of year with the temperature going into the twenties, and it is hard to imagine that we are going slowly but surely into the winter season. I find it kind of a sad time, because the summer is now past and only the memories of it remain with the photographs taken being an aid that are able to instantly bring us back to the time frame the picture was taken. It makes me aware of the passing time and the inability to hold onto it even if I wish it so. One could compare time to a steamroller operated by a cruel driver who doesn't seem to be aware of people's anguish, fears and frustrations. Some people may call me a coward because I am somewhat afraid of the future and no doubt one should live from day to day and in some cases from hour to hour, as we don't know when the grim reaper appears, possibly out of nowhere. As I look at the trees outside my window, I realize that they too need to preserve themselves for next spring, and the reason for the leaves to be so colourful is because the tree is shutting down and is withholding the sap to the leaf that it needs to sustain itself and so the leaf is basically drying out ergo, the colouring process and eventually the leaf falls to the ground to become food for the next generation of grass, plants or trees. I thought about the possibility that it is the leaf itself that shuts off in order to make sure that there is continuity not only for the tree but also for the next generation of leaves. Because where the leaf was attached tot he tree branch a slight bump or swelling will appear which is the start of a new bud. How wondrous it all is in our eyes and we stand in awe over the mysteries of life as in life-force. Like time itself there is no stopping it, there is even life in decaying substances. I cannot help believe that there is a greater force at work here and that I therefore, must reject the possibility that all life form happened by chance. I realize that this is only my opinion, but when I see all the evidence I cannot come to any other conclusion.

The creative forces are in their own way ruled by other forces that limits each creation to their own boundaries, beyond which they cannot go.

Therefore I believe that the Creator Himself is at the helm of all what we can survey and perceive, with our limited knowledge and perception of things. When we are young the world and all it's attractions was always beckoning us to come and participate in it's fun and entertainment and I dare say most of us did do exactly that and unless there comes a time in our life that makes us stop and think what our being on earth is all about, we will go on doing precisely that, to our own detriment, I may add. Because the world loves it's own. The person who is in the world will not become a listener to the quiet voice that can be heard when all becomes still around us, the world will drown it out. Heaven above and the world below, as the expression goes. I know what the world below is but what is "Heaven above." To some heaven above are the stars, the galaxies and planets of every sort, black holes etc. But I don't think that it means that. Heaven is where the Creator is with His Son the Christ and the Holy Spirit, where all the angels are,, the ultimate place of worship where no uncleanness is nor allowed, where pureness reigns, where there is an indescribable love which surrounds everything, where the laughter of true happiness is heard and the praising of the Creator, His Son and the Holy Spirit, don't ever have an end. Our spirit soars to unbelievable heights, where elation is constant, where there is no want of anything no sorrows no tears except for joy, the ultimate bliss. Who can ignore such a place, by staying in this worldly plain? Let us therefore strive for righteousness and throw off the bands that keep us chained to the world, so that we may become a new creature, heaven bound through Jesus Christ our Lord.

THE STRANGER THAT HE KNEW

It was a very safe and secure place where he was in this world. From his high vantage point he could see all around and was above most people. Below in the valley of life he could see the people struggle in their every day life, he also could hear the anguish cries of children, the sobs of the lonely the helpless and the poor in spirit. There seem to be a constant battle going on down there and sometimes shots rang out and he was glad that he had his own rifle for protection with lots of shells with their shiny bullets. He had given some of them names, there was "pain and suffering" and the one he had called "terminator" and let's not forget "eraser". He also had a bow and arrows, he also had given names to the arrows, like "despair," "humiliation," "anger" "spite" to name a few and then there was the one he liked best called "don't come near me." Yes he was well prepared for any eventuality, nobody was going to get to him, besides he was well protected by the two walls he had put up, the first one was "Ignorance", the smaller one that he had put up right behind it, was "Indifference." The food supply he had up there, was hidden away of course, it would last him a lifetime, no need to share with those down in the valley of despair. He had all kinds of canned food that he could eat at a moments notice, there were cans of self-indulgence, "pride," "self-pity," some "home made love" and some cans of "Holier then Thou." He also had bottled water from the "what do you care" company that tasted great, he also had some bottles of wine for medicinal purposes of course, brand named "never enough." No he was well off and he thanked God on his bare knees every night before going into his bed called "ego," for everything .Then came the day it happened. The day had started off well enough the sun was shining and there was not a cloud (worry) in the sky. As he took up his guard post by the wall because even though the people in the valley knew enough not to try anything against him, you never know, there could be someone who may try. Imagine his surprise when he saw somebody way down the bottom of the hill starting to come up. Quickly he grabbed his rifle and was about to fire a few rounds when he realized that there was something vaguely familiar about the person coming up. He could not put his finger on it, at the same time it seemed to get a little darker which was strange after all this was mid morning.

Again he looked over the wall of ignorance and sure enough this person was still coming, he could see him a little better now as he looked through the binoculars of his minds' eye. The man was old and grey, his hair was matted to his forehead and he looked very, very tired, his clothes were no more than tattered rags and were in desperate need of repair, his white flesh showing through the rags. He still did not recognize him, curiously though, the closer he got the darker it became. The old man stopped more and more often to rest and he was getting more and more curious as to who that person was. He shouted down to him but he did not seem to hear him, the closer he got the more sorry he felt for that old man he was after all in a desperate pitiful state. The darkness was starting to affect him now, and being used to full daylight ,he admittedly became a little scared. The man was almost to the top, to where he was. He could barely see him now, something seemed to affect his eyesight. When at last he looked up at him he realized that this man in his tattered rags, his grey matted hair and poor condition was his "soul" that was about to leave him. All of a sudden he wished he had been different in life, he also came to the realization that it was too late for that, as his time had come. He grabbed a hold of that old man, shook him and asked him "why are you in such a sorry state!" The old man said to him "because you made me so."

ABOUT TRUST

What is trust? It's amazing how trusting we are under certain circumstances. We tend to reason within ourselves as to how great a trust we may put in certain things or people. Take for instance a doctor in the medical profession that we have to see for one thing or another, the trust we put in that man borders on the amazing. If he were to say, take off your shirt or blouse, we immediately comply with that request with no hesitation at all or if he asks to bare all we will do just that. So you see that we tend to put our trust in people that we think know what they are doing. The same goes when we are purchasing a car be it second hand or new. In the first instance the car salesman will tell you in glowing terms how good the vehicle is and shows you the new tires, no rust, the clean interior etc. You then proceed to purchase the car because you trust the car salesman, only to find out about the things he did not tell you about, I guess you could call that misplaced trust. If we were to purchase a new car we put our trust in a lot of things and people. We trust that the car is free of defects after all it is new and that the plant workers did not forget to tighten any bolts or screws and you trust that the advertisement about the vehicle is not misleading and that the engine is the best money can buy. It is called trusting the product. Trust and believe are quite often put in the same category. Unless we believe, there can be no trust, ergo trust has believe built into it. If after a week of really cold weather the lake has frozen over we may think that the ice will hold us. By gauging the thickness of the ice and having taken into account the week of freezing weather we trust our judgement and walk on the frozen water carefully at first and then as our confidence in our judgement increases we grow more and more bold and venture farther and farther from the shore. If however the ice where to break under our feet and we found ourselves up to our waist in cold muddy water, the confidence in our ability to judge the ice thickness maybe severely impaired and so will be our trust in that ability. I guess the next time we like to go for a walk on the ice it may well be a challenge to our courage. The Americans have as their motto "In God we trust" which is a very powerful motto indeed. Blessed is that nation that put their trust in the Almighty, they will never be defeated, as the Lord will not allow it, because he is true to his promises.

In the second world war the German soldier had on his belt buckle the inscription "Gott mit uns" basically meaning "God is on our side". At the height of Hitler's power Germany had stopped to be a God fearing nation on the whole and Satan ruled Germany through Hitler and his henchmen and inflicted untold grief upon many a nation. Their God was Satan and Germany could not win the war because in the end, good will always prevail over evil. I realize that Russia, a nation that suffered more then any other nation from nazi Germany was the catalyst in the defeat of Germany even if they were not a God-fearing nation, but God used them in combination with the United States, England, France and the other allies to defeat Germany. Russia however had expansionism on its mind and occupied a lot of the eastern European countries but as we saw in the last decade it all went by the wayside because God cannot be on the side of a nation that does not put their trust in Him.

ABOUT TRUST

AN ODE OR TWO

On the wings of thought
Our loved ones come
Through memory, to give to some
Encouragement we need
On the road we travel
For some the pavement is smooth
For others it is gravel
Be not dismayed look up at Him
Who is your Maker
He's able to make you too
Through His son partaker
Of that heavenly realm
We may obtain through grace
Which is our goal in life
So we may once embrace
Our source of happiness
The Christ, God bless.

HONOURING AMERICA

Oh America I honour thee
That land belonging to the free
Your soil brought forth such fine young men
That fought in Europe's wars and then
Tried to forget the things they'd seen
And wished the wars had never been
The comrades lost brought heartfelt pain
The scars from war wounds that remain
Are proof of heroism and of valour
So are the medals in the parlour
They are for every one to see
Let's not forget this, is my plea
Although I am Canadian
I bow my head in thanks
To all those fine young men.

ABOUT IRELAND

Oh Ireland thou land of beauty, thou be called Emerald Isle for thou art set as a precious stone amidst the deep blue ocean who's waves are caressing thy shores on every side. Thou art a separate land, unique in thy own way as are thy people. In thee be found a remnant of one of the lost tribes of Israel that settled on thy shores so long ago.

It is now generally an accepted fact that Celts are the descendants of one or more of the tribes of Israel that settled all through Europe in places like Finland, Norway, Denmark, Sweden, Germany, The Netherlands, Ireland, Scotland, England, France, Spain, Greece and others. While listening to Gene Scott who was a pastor in Los Angeles (but since passed away) who was an expert on the lost tribes of Israel. From him I found out that the two daughters of Zedikiah, the last king of Judah, survived the massacre of the royal house because they were female and were taken by Jeremiah the prophet to Western Europe where one married the king of Ireland and the other the king of Spain. In all this we can see the hand of the Almighty who had promised David king of Israel that at the second coming of Christ one of his descendents would be sitting on a throne ruling over a nation. Through intermarriage the Queen of England is a direct descendant of the house of David as are all the royal houses of Europe via intermarriage. It is not surprising that so many male offspring in Ireland are named after Jeremiah. This short explanation may shock many an Irishman but it shows the unique role Ireland has played in the fulfillment of Gods promises. Ireland has suffered tremendously in the past especially during the potato famine of the 1840 ties that cost the lives of millions of people because of starvation and related diseases and resulted in the great emigration movement to America, Canada and other countries like Australia and New Zealand. The Irish are a tenacious race of people and their men make for excellent soldiers because of this trait and seem to have a fearlessness about them which stem from the fact that they were raised that way for many generations. The fathers would instil into their sons the fact that they were male and no sissy stuff would be allowed and to stand up to anyone who would disagree or beg to differ on a certain matter even if it had to come to blows. There is nothing wrong with that in a sense, but the Irish have made it a way of life. The expression "the fighting Irish" is well known around the world I guess, so I don't have to elaborate.

The Irish are a clan oriented people with strong family ties and are loyal through thick and thin. It is very sad to see that because of religious affiliation brother has been fighting brother for the past hundred years. It was thought that the separation of political units in 1921 would bring an end to the violence but it did not. The separation of Northern Ireland from the rest of the nation only brought more intense hatred between the Roman-Catholics and the Protestants with sectarian killings and maiming being the order of the day. I don't believe that a true Roman-Catholic or a true Protestant would participate I this sort of thing, as neither church would condone actions of this kind. Recently efforts have started to reunite Ireland to be again one nation in which people would get along with each-other regardless as to what church they belong to or what their political affiliation is. It would be a slow process because of an inbred hatred that was passed from father to son for so many generations. There are very few families that were not touched by the violence of the past and I hope for the sake of all the Irish people this will be successful because they deserve better then this sapping of strength through separation. Irishmen and woman will be able to look at each-other without wondering whether the person they are looking at is Catholic or Protestant. The expression "blessed are the hate-mongers" is not anywhere in the bible

But "Blessed are the Peacemakers" is. May all that labour towards that end be blessed indeed.

ABOUT MY DAD

June 1 1997

It is not surprising that in the past few months I have come face to face with my mortality. I guess one reason is because of the death of my beloved father through cancer in November 1996. I always thought the man to be indestructible. He was very strong willed, strong minded with a very strong body. To me these three things are necessary for a long and healthy life. My dad died at the age of 86 and had lived an examplinary life style and could be a role model for many a person, he was generous to a fault and was never slow to help someone in need no matter who it was. I feel ashamed for not having written about him earlier as he was worthy of praise by everyone especially by me as I am his oldest son. He was a truly religious person and made no bones about as to how he felt about things because they were dear to his heart. He was an honest and truthful man in whom there was no guile, who was led by his conscience, it being the inner voice of the Creator. Naturally there are always people ready to point out the errors made by an individual like my father just to prove that he was not perfect in every way. It is for me a certainty that in his last few hours on this earth the love of Christ was present because my father was a faithful servant to the end even though he was in agony because of the cancer that had consumed his pancreas and other vital organs. It must have been a very lonely moment for him because it was after midnight with nobody around but the night nurse who heard him cry out that he was dying. I hope that the Comforter the Holy Spirit was present when my dad needed it most because God will not abandon those who call upon His name in their hour of need because He said he would and God is not a liar. Needless to say that a person who dies in the Lord will be blessed for all eternity as they will not see death because death is swallowed up because of what Christ did for people like that. His Spirit implanted in those people will quicken their mortal bodies at the sound of the trumpet on judgment day to put on immortality not to be judged but to be with Christ as they are like Christ. Christ will not be judged by anyone and because they are in

Christ and Christ is in them and they are one. Those that have come this far will stand in awe and realize that only the grace of God made this possible and nothing that they did except perhaps that they truly believed in Gods word and with the help of the Holy Spirit did understand and saw the reason for their existence.

It is a great wonder to the new born again Christian and will probably be wondering why he or she was picked, being the greatest of all sinners, however when the truth of it all starts to sink in him or her they will give thanksgiving to the Creator from the morning until the evening because of the miracle wrought in him and be called a child of God. This is a great mystery to most people and most of us will never come to the knowledge of Christ and his atoning work because our minds are closed and we are blinded by unbelief as Satan will not let go of us lest we would see and be converted. Christ already spoke of this during His stay on earth. Another mystery is the fact that all the born again Christians were chosen from the beginning of time before the worlds were formed. This being the case it follows that all the souls of man were in existence at what we call the beginning of time. As you can see as to the what's and why's there is no end the mystery deepens the more we get into this and for every answer we may have there are more questions. We as human beings are part of this great mystery, which will be revealed to everyone at the proper time. Most people have come to realize that we are living in the last days, the deterioration of morality in today's modern world is like it was in the days of Noah and even though Noah preached for 80 years only he himself and his family were saved from the flood that came upon the earth. The generation of today is a generation of pleasure seekers, they have become lovers of themselves, cold-hearted and seem to be without natural affection for their fellow man. I am aware that the same traits are in me and to deny this is folly the only difference may well be the fact that I am aware of them, while they are not. Often enough I ask the Creator of all things, to give me a fleshly heart and to take away this heart of stone that weighs me down so much at times We buried our stepmother last Wednesday the 28th of May after a relatively short bout with cancer. Only God who understands the hearts of man knows why this happened, may He have had mercy on her soul and given her the experience of the saving grace of Christ in her last hours on this earth.

THE PAST

While watching the movie "Love is a many splendored thing" I was actually looking into the past as I saw William Holden and Jennifer Jones holding hands, kissing and doing all the other things that people in love do, even though it is according to a script they have to follow. He was ever so handsome in those days and she was very beautiful. They are both gone now and because they are, I felt a tremendous sadness in me and a universal love towards them because they looked so real on the screen as if they were still alive. They still did cast a shadow on the hillside that beautiful morning when they met under the big tree on top of the hill overlooking Hong Kong harbour, they could still feel and touch each-other and express their love by saying the words. Why this sadness is in me I don't really know, maybe it is because I am on the same road that they were on which eventually leads to ones demise, it is just a question as to when. I wish it was not so and that I could magically make them alive again, to again experience the world around them. Alas this is not possible as we cannot turn back the clock The endlessness of it all boggles the mind and we are only in part able to understand the wisdom of the Almighty by Whom there is no time and were the "truth" in it's true meaning is absolute. We are what we are by His mercy alone and the very reason for our existence is only to become part of Him through Jesus Christ His son who because of His unspeakable love for the human race, laid down His life for the chosen ones who were found worthy to live with Him eternally. Nobody really knows about the eternal things, Paul says that we are looking through a dark glass but one day we will see it face to face. Paul compares us as to a ship laden in the harbour of life ready to depart to a different life, which will be determined by the load we bring with us. I hope with all my heart that the hope that his in me does not leave me empty handed, as I believe in Jesus Christ and His atoning work. May it be known that I "fall off the wagon" often enough and need forgiveness for my sins on a daily basis almost hourly as it were.

RELIGIOUS THOUGHTS, STORIES AND POETRY

Recently I had occasion to visit a sick friend of mine and when I saw the suffering of many a patient I was overcome with love for those people and wished I could relieve their suffering by words or deeds and wanted to embrace them and say to them how sorry I am for their condition and that everything will the alright.

Praying for the sick must be everyone's duty for his fellow man.

To me it is a very sad thing not being able to ease the pain that so many people are saddled with in this world, like the apostles did when they first were preaching the Word after receiving the Holy Spirit, not for self gratification but only for the honour of the Almighty and to prove His power over everything including sicknesses and deformities of any kind and to use this as a tool to bring people to repentance. The faith that is in me may not be strong enough to be obeyed by an illness or disease to leave the body of the afflicted person because of a fear of failure. By writing this I seem to affirm a weakness in my faith and could be likened unto Peter the apostle who denied his master 3 times in one night and cried bitterly afterwards. Who am I to infringe on such a powerful source unless it is given me in my heart to do so? It would be a tremendous honour to be found worthy to do an act of healing not for myself but for a fellow human being in need of it. As we walk the path of life we would be well advised to give from ourselves to others without expecting anything in return. For we have received freely and must give freely to receive more abundantly. Those who are allowed to drink from the well of wisdom will find that true happiness comes through the giving, which must become second nature to us and is actually contrary to our nature as we are according to the "Good Book" haters of God and our fellow man. Only a profound change in us through Jesus Christ our Lord will give us a different outlook on life and our fellow man. We will be taught this through the Holy Spirit because we will have become one with our Saviour and our path will be well lit and all our needs for the now and for the eternal will be taken care of, we will be free of worry about ourselves and will be waiting with impatience for our departure from this life and without angst, to be with Him who made it all possible for us the greatest of all sinners who have received mercy without end.

RELENTLESS

The winter of 1998 was a very mild one in more than one way. Record high temperatures were set on an almost daily basis. It also brought a lot of grief to many people in Quebec and in eastern Ontario when the ice storm occurred in the early part of this year. Many people were cut off from the rest of the world because of the downed power lines, which in some cases were not restored until 4 weeks after the ice storm causing an awful lot of hardship. Now everything is back to normal for those people but I am sure that this subject will come up in many a conversation during the next few years. It's now April and the temperatures are in the sixties although we've had a few frosty nights. The trees are budding now and the Irises, Tulips, Lilies, Hyacinths and all other flowers are working their way out of the ground and there is no stopping them, for whom can stop the spring from coming who is so powerful but God alone. I am amazed at the relentlessness of it all, that force that is called "nature" which brings renewal to all the growing plants, shrubs and trees as well as in the animal world, with the birth of a new generation of animals in this northern hemisphere. We stand in awe when we behold it all and with our thoughts we thank the Creator for His presence. We as a people could use the Easter season to reflect on the fact that Christ died for us on the cross to take away our sins. We too could take part in this renewal by being as it were a new creation like the new born animals, almost like a fresh start and throw off all that which is a deterrent in the obtaining of internal life. Let's love our enemies and bless those that speak evil of us and do us harm, knowing that these people are in the employ of that evil one and will have their reward. With our minds eye we can see the end for these people and have pity on them. We can also do ourselves a favour by stopping to smoke cigarettes if we did or if we tend to over indulge in the consumption of alcohol to stop drinking or if we were inclined to overeat to cut down on our eating habits as these things tend to be detrimental to our physical as well as our mental health. Which could lead to an early stay in a" home" or another place where we don't want to be. The extension of our life expectancy may well be the key to the Kingdom because some of us need all the time we can have to become a born again Christian.

Printed in Canada